Blood in the Streets
Dr. Gary Ray

ISBN: 979-8-9906692-2-2 | Library of Congress No. 2025927270

E-book: ISBN 979-8-9906692-3-9

Scripture quotations marked KJV from the King James Version of the Bible.

Scripture quotations marked NKJV are from the New King James Version Copyright 1979, 1980, 1982 Thomas Nelson. All rights reserved.

Scripture quotations marked ESV English Standard Version® Copyright 2001 by Crossway.

Scripture's quotations marked NIV taken from the Holy Bible, New International Version®. Copyright © 1973, 1978, 1984 International Bible Society. Used by permission of Zondervan. All rights reserved.

Scripture quotations marked NLT taken from Holy Bible, New Living Translation. Copyright © 1996, 2004, 2007 by Tyndale House Foundation. Used by permission of Tyndale House Publishers Inc., Carol Stream, Illinois 60188. All rights reserved. New Living, NLT, and the New Living Translation logo are registered trademarks of Tyndale House Publishers.

To order additional copies, please visit: https://www.drgaryray.com

When you order directly from Gary, **he will sign it and ship it!**

Painters Dream Productions is a Book Publisher dedicated to providing publishing services at affordable prices, helping to elevate our Author's work. https://www.PaintersDream.com (931) 304-1359

GARY RAY MINISTRIES

Painters Dream PRODUCTIONS

Website Design | Audio Video Production | Social Media Marketing | Book Publishing

TABLE OF CONTENTS

Ophelia McDowell Ray
(October 10, 1950 – November 10, 2025)

I wanted to write something in this book to honor my beautiful wife of 54 years who, on the 10th of November, passed from this life to her heavenly reward.

You know, as I begin to write this to go in my new book, I'm taken to John chapter 11. It's where Mary and Martha's brother Lazarus was sick. Martha, you know, called 911! No, really, they called for Jesus to come, but He didn't, and Lazarus died. They had to bury their beloved brother. I know how they felt because in February, when she was diagnosed with pancreatic cancer, we prayed. I have so many wonderful, wonderful Christian brothers and friends and sisters and wonderful children who have been right by my side. I couldn't have made it without them. Friends prayed and prayed for God to heal her, but we didn't get the answer that we wanted at the time. I realized the day after the funeral, when I stood by her grave gazing at the graveside and oh how I missed her!

But standing there, Jesus spoke into my spirit; "don't weep my son, for I heard your prayers, and I gave her the ultimate healing. She's safe at home".

He gave me a mandate and it's that I must live my life and do the work that I promised her I would do until I go to that same place. Well, I am at peace now, I really am. Oh yes, I miss her terribly. I go into the bedroom, and I can still smell her. It's still in her clothes, but yeah, I know where she is. Yes, she received the ultimate healing and now she's at home with Jesus and I have the joy of knowing that I will soon see her when my time here is completed.

I want to send blessings to all those who stood with me in prayer and who have supported me, thank you so much. I love every one of you.

Charlie Kirk
(1993 - 2025)

What Charlie's death proved was my book was right on time. Charlie was assassinated, and it was political. I grieve not only for his death or for the wonderful, lovely family that he left, but I'm grieving for America. From the beginning of time, in the book of Genesis, we had offered to us one of the greatest gifts.

In the garden, because of sin, their innocence was lost and ever since then, mankind paid the price of the sin. Later, even Israel couldn't seem to get it all together and today neither do we, so it seems.

HOWEVER, by the grace of God, knowing ALL THINGS, it was as if He thought "I am the ONLY ONE Who can pay the price for sin" and then proceed to pay while cancelling all our sins on the cross.

Like the father of lies, the serpent of old, I think the individual who committed this murder did not realize that he was unleashing a fire that would burn hotter and farther than Charlie could have imagined.

If the devil knew that Christ on the cross was going to give us eternal life, he would have never participated at all. But even he is under obedience (Job) just like we are. PRAISE GOD!

After I watched Charlie's wife, Erika speak during the press conference just 24 hours after his passing. I understood that the Turning Point organization that has already had a huge impact on our country will be even brighter to the dark and dying world. I'm sure that all these communist organizations will try again and yes, we will see more blood in the streets. **It is going to come.**

Whether we choose to believe or not, or if we bury our heads in the sand, still it's going to happen, and then the end will come. The Father will look at His Son and say "go bring my children home."

The GREATEST NEWS OF ALL is that you are either going to read this entire book, or He is going to bring you home either way YOU WIN!

GARY RAY
MINISTRIES

ADVANCE REVIEWS

I would first like to say it's an honor to support a man with a message and a mission such as Rev. Gary Ray. Brother Gary is a true example of what Jesus told the church to do and that is to GO into all the world and preach the Gospel and to bring the Truth to a dying generation in the last days and this book you hold in your hand is Revelation knowledge of the events Jesus said would be taking place in this last hour of time. This information is vital to the believer and if you are a Pastor or an Evangelist or a Child of God that loves God, Family, and Country, I highly recommend you get a copy not just for yourself but for your parishioners as well and all of those that support and follow your ministry. So now get ready to watch the pages of this book come alive as the End time is coming to pass right before your eyes. May God richly bless you.

Bishop Steve Warren
Faith Chapel Ministries

Congratulations to our good friend, Dr. Gary Ray, on the release of your new book "Blood in the Streets." Karen and I truly believe that if there was ever a timely word for the Church, <u>this is it</u>. This book is a must-read for anyone seeking an honest, eye-opening look at the current condition of the Church and our deep need for a genuine outpouring of the Holy Spirit in our world once again. We love you, Dr. Ray, and our prayer is that the Holy Spirit will continue to use you in a powerful and life-changing way.

Mark & Karen Poff
New Harvest Ministries – Kingsport, TN

"Blood in the Streets", is Dr. Ray's third book. He has a heart for the Church and strives to present to the body of Christ, messages that the Holy Spirit drops into his Spirit. After careful perusal of "Blood in the Streets", I am sure the reader will be challenged! With great depth and willingness to present the truth, Dr. Ray has exhausted all means possible to stir the heart of the reader! See what is ahead! Look at prophecy fulfilled! This book will speak volumes about our future. Come, walk through this journey with Dr. Ray and wait in anticipation for the next book he drops on your heart!

Dr. Bobby Howard

"Blood in the Streets." may be Dr. Gary Ray's most timely work ever. It's a warning, a message for the church, to the state and yes, a warning be ready...A must read.

Lem Kinslow

A NOTE FROM THE PUBLISHER

Our prayer is that as you turn these pages, you will hear not just Gary's voice, but the Lord's call to renew, restore, and strengthen His people. When you pick up this book, you'll notice right away that Gary doesn't dress up his words in stiff formality—he writes the way he talks. His roots run deep in the South, and his voice carries the rhythms and plain-spoken wisdom of his heritage.

But don't mistake his storytelling style for light reading. His words are both a mirror and a challenge. He loves the church too much to leave it where it is, and he isn't afraid to call us to rise higher, dig deeper, and walk closer with the Lord.

This is not a book of theory written from an ivory tower. It's written from the pews and pulpits, from conversations on front porches and church steps, from a lifetime of watching where the church has been faithful—and where it has faltered.

We believe his message is timely, urgent, and worth sitting with. He invites us, in his own way, to "come on in, sit a spell, and reckon with what God might be saying to us."

Painters Dream
PRODUCTIONS

Website Design | Audio Video Production | Social Media Marketing | Book Publishing

CHAPTER 1:
A Warning

I must say this in the beginning, I'm not writing this book to alarm you, but I am writing it to arm you, so that the church can once again become victorious.

What I am writing in this book is real. It's not make believe, there are real things going on in our world that should scare <u>every</u> Christian.

I've said it many times, and I'll say it again, if you want to know what's going on, read "The Communist Manifesto" and you begin to see what's really happening. Our cities are in trouble, and I still believe that **the only answer is the Church**. As we begin this book, my prayer is that it will awaken you.

The word "blood" is mentioned around 700 times in the Bible, with the first reference in Genesis 4:10 and the last in Revelation 19:13. The Bible also mentions "bloody" 16 times.

> *I will send a plague against you and blood will be spilled in your streets. The attack will come from every direction and your people will lie slaughtered within your walls. Then everyone will know that I am the Lord.* EZEKIEL 28:23 (NLT)

> *In your streets flowed the blood of the prophets and of God's holy people and the blood of people slaughtered all over the world."* REVELATION 18:24 (NLT)

Jerusalem, once so full of people, is now deserted. She who was once great among the nations now sits alone like a widow. Once the queen of all the earth, she is now a slave. She sobs through the night; tears stream down her cheeks. Among all her lovers, there is no one left to comfort her. All her friends have betrayed her and become her enemies.
Lamentations 1:1-2 (NLT)

As we go further in this book, you will find something that was in my last book "Behind the Veil" because the condition of the church determines when the blood in the streets will begin to flow. And this book, you will find is a sequel to my second book, "Behind the Veil: A true picture of the Church."

I will write in this book some very difficult things that we have had a vision of what is really happening in our world today. Some things are very hard to say while praying and seeking God's face. I realize to what lengths the devil, our adversary, will go to stop the truth from being told; I am truly convinced that my wife's cancer diagnosis is a direct attempt by the devil to stop this book from being written.

I will even tell you this; there are people within the confines of the Christian church who don't want this written, because brothers and sisters, **the church is a part of the problem.**

I tend to write about difficult things within the confines of the church. I just became aware of a new one for me, it is called sensationalism, in religious circles. These believers use the melodramatic, they use over-the-top theatrical methods in their religious services.

They are overblown, and there are incredible claims in religious literature. We find a religious sensationalist can be either one who manipulates others through such methods, or a wide-eyed participant mesmerized by the thrill of it all.

Long ago, there was a pastor in Germany who began to realize what was happening to his country; killing 6 million Jews and destroying the country, this man knew what they were doing and what was about to happen.

They had him taken to a concentration camp. As they were stringing him up, he could hear the Allied armies coming. Another two hours and he could've been saved, but they killed him so that they could continue their destructive tactics to destroy a nation. People, we must wake up. It's happening again.

We no longer want to hear the truth; we just want our ears tickled. We just want to hear good things, but Church, war and destruction are imminent.

You've heard me talk about the deep state, that there are individuals pulling the strings and telling Democratic leaders what to do. It's sad but true, these individuals don't want our world to succeed. They have what I like to call a hidden agenda.

If we go back to the beginning, the Jewish nation experienced some of the same things that took them into captivity. Now let us come on down to where Germany tried to extinguish the Jewish nation. Of course, we have been taught that the devil is behind it all.

But what does the Bible say?

The One forming light and creating darkness, causing well-being and creating calamity; **I am the Lord who does all these**. Isaiah 45:7

We must understand that NOTHING is outside God's purview.

Please understand this is the Bible, not just my belief. If I am right, the return of Jesus could be very soon. I have come to the realization that preparation means everything in this day. As I have stated, as I went through cancer with my wife, you can't let what you're going through stop you from doing what you're called to do.

I do believe, quite possibly, that the son of perdition may already be alive and could soon appear. No one knows the schedule that God has put in place for the end times to begin, I don't know and no one else knows.

Again, I'm truly convinced that my wife's cancer diagnosis is a direct attempt by the devil to stop this book from being written. As you can see, God had different plans. I did not get a revelation from God telling me this, it's what I'm personally convinced of. So, even though the enemy was bored, and had nothing to do and decided to present himself to heaven, and God said, "have you considered my servant Ophelia".

Sometimes the things that I feel, and sense in the spirit, can be a little bit on the frightening side. Over my 41 years of full-time ministry, I have learned to trust what I sense in the spirit or what I know that I hear from God.

I will never say "God said it", unless I know for sure that God said it, and in the same sense, we can't push aside when the Spirit of God speaks, especially when it concerns certain things that are soon to happen.

It's challenging sometimes to put these things on pen and paper, but it's necessary. Sometimes we just must stop and pray and trust the Lord with what we feel. Let me say this here; you can't worship God from a distance, you must become a participant, you must be washed in the Spirit to enjoy the anointing that accompanies salvation.

Now, let's talk about a nation that has forgotten its God. The church that we see now has taken on an appearance that is more like the world than the Church. We are now seeing a perverted gospel. It's not real, it's not good news.

We wonder why we cannot see miraculous things happening in church. We once did. Once when I was building the church in Florida, I had a lady come in one night and close to the end of the service.

As I was on the altar praying with people, I asked if there was anyone here who needed healing. A young lady came to the front and said, "I need healing" she indicated that she had just been diagnosed with cancer.

I asked her if she believed that God could heal her. She said "yes." I prayed, and this is what I said. I asked God to heal the sister of cancer and let there not be any sign, not even a scar that the cancer was ever there. Three weeks later she came back to church and gave a testimony.

Please remember what I said when I prayed for her. She said when the doctor came in after running the tests now, he said she had a biopsy that had left a scar, but that he could not even find the scar. It was as if the cancer was never there. **This is God**.

I'm giving this testimony to you to say there is healing now. It's because we have perverted the miraculous things of God, I will go as far as to say, we have perverted the gifts. Understand that they cannot work because of their perversion. They become nothing more than being just like the world. They are glorifying themselves more than God, calling themselves more like the Pope with their large, independent ministries, and still, they will not honor God.

I believe that I wrote this book "Blood in the Streets" simply because the church will not take its rightful position and do what God has called it to be and do. I am convinced that things will not change until Jesus returns.

But, praise God, there is a beautiful remnant church that is still prevalent in America. They are small, and they are scattered, but this is what we see now, and there doesn't seem to be any signs of being different. One reason that they cannot grow is because they are not mentoring young men and women, helping them to grow in the Word, and becoming spiritually strong in the Word.

There was a minister who wrote a book, "We Have Yet Not Many Fathers." The premise of the book was that we're not growing men and women and teaching them how to reach others and seeing lost souls brought into the Kingdom of God.

This morning in service at the church, God brought to our attention the prodigals; they have yet to come home.

These are our children, far from God, they have become a part of this Z generation. They have embraced the thought that it does not matter if there is a God and He doesn't care about them. Yet we know that He does.

Yet, you and I both know this is not true. We see them now embracing LGBTQ. (I detest using capital letters to describe them.) And then there is gender reassignment that says if they want to change from a girl to a boy or a boy to a girl, it doesn't matter to what they were born as. Evidently, they don't realize that whatever DNA they were born with is the same DNA they will have when they die. You cannot change your DNA.

Maybe the hyper grace theory that God has forgiven their sins past, present, and future, regardless of their state of salvation, or repentance, means there's no need to worry. But we know that we must confess our known sins to God, and He will be faithful to forgive us of all our sins, known and unknown. In 1 John we see:

> *But if we walk in the light as He is in the light, we have fellowship with one another, and the blood of Jesus Christ His Son cleanses us from all sin. 1 John 1:7*

> *If we confess our sins, He is faithful and righteous, so that He will forgive us our sins and cleanse us from all unrighteousness. 1 John 1:9*

And you, being dead in your trespasses and the uncircumcision of your flesh, He has made alive together with Him, having forgiven you all trespasses, having wiped out the handwriting of requirements that was against us, which was contrary to us. And He has taken it out of the way, having nailed it to the cross. Colossians 2:13-14

I write to you, little children, because your sins are forgiven you for His name's sake. 1 John 2:12

To Him all the prophets witness that, through His name, whoever believes in Him will receive remission of sins. Acts 10:43

The only way that we solve this problem is to saturate ourselves with the word of the living God. I believe at this point that there's a scripture that you need to hear it is

It is a fearful thing to fall into the hands of the living God. Hebrews 10:31.

I believe if we read Ezekiel, and Lamentations, just the first two verses are enough to see a picture of what the world looks like today. You can also see what Christians look like today, and what they are acting like. Based on what I'm seeing in the Bible concerning their actions, there is a price they will pay for their behavior, and it's found in a Psalm of David.

The earth is the LORD's, and everything in it.

The world and all its people belong to him. For he laid the earth's foundation on the seas and built it on the ocean depths. Who may climb the mountain of the LORD? Who may stand in his holy place? Only those whose hands and hearts are pure, who do not worship idols and never tell lies.

They will receive the LORD's blessing and have a right relationship.

At first, I wondered if God was allowing America to experience this because of our actions against Israel. As I got deeper into the Scriptures, I no longer wondered, but now I know, America is experiencing this because they have become just as disobedient as Israel was then.

By allowing our enemies to take control, and we know who our enemies are, I am convinced that they are in Washington. It is called the swamp, or the deep state, and they are controlling our nation.

You will hear through this book, multiple times, a phrase:

"When will the church in America wake up?"

The condition of the church today is a reflection of what we've been building on for a long time now.

CHAPTER 2:
Perilous Times

God has allowed us to come to this place because of our disobedience. I firmly believe it is the church, not denominations, not a building, not numbers, <u>but the church</u>. We know that the church is internal, it is in our physical being, it **is not the building** that we attend every Sunday. That is merely a building, if you were to strike a match to that building it would burn to the ground, but His kingdom is what we, the Church, should be concerned with.

I am convinced the only hope this world has, is for the church to wake up, and for Christians to realize that it is time to take up our weapons. They're not carnal, but they are spiritual, and they are powerful in the hands of a blood bought Christian. Just let me give you the scripture to prove that.

> *For though we walk in the flesh, we do not war according to the flesh. For the weapons of our warfare are not carnal but mighty in God for pulling down strongholds, casting down arguments and every high thing that exalts itself against the knowledge of God, bringing every thought into captivity to the obedience of Christ, and being ready to punish all disobedience when your obedience is fulfilled.*
> 2 CORINTHIANS 10:3-5 (NKJV)

And as I read Scripture, I see a word that looms at me, it's called flesh. As I begin to see the church, it's not spiritual any longer. Let's look at this. Out of 100 people, one will read the Bible, 99 will read the Christian. Wow! I bet that got your attention.

It is a fleshly church operating on feelings and emotions, which is the flesh, not the Spirit. Then I realized that they have tasted the earthly substance, but never the heavenly substance. It's called flesh, and it's spiritual. God is still looking for a people that He can trust and allow them to be leaders in the Church.

God has out lasted our plans, and I found out that God really loves to interrupt our plans because they only lead us into sin. I've been hearing a lot lately about a great revival that is coming into the church world, and I have to say that I really doubt it.

There are too many self-called prophets trying to enlighten us on what God is or isn't going to do. The only thing I am going to say is that when you say, "God said" they better KNOW He said it. Oh yes, I think there will be breakouts here and there but the revival that these men talk about has already taken place. And we need to get the correct definition for the word revival. Its meaning has nothing to do with getting people saved from the lake of fire.

The word saved has more than one meaning. As does the word revive:

> *Then we will not turn away from you; revive us, and we will call on your name. Restore us, LORD God Almighty; make your face shine on us, that we may be saved.*
> Psalm 80:18

Normally when you call a meeting for the purpose of a revival, it's only to revive the church. This definitely needs to happen in the Church, but it has not happened to this point, that's for sure.

The church truly needs to be revived before we see the worst, more blood running in the streets of our cities. The Church must be revived, in other words, the Church needs to become alive once again.

I believe that God can release men again to do the work of the Kingdom. I'm talking about real Kingdom business, not playtime then many will ask the question.

"What is Kingdom business"? Let me explain the difference between the Church and the Kingdom. First, the Church is internal, the church is **in you**, in all reality you are the Church.

> *Do you not know that you are a temple of God and that the Spirit of God dwells in you?* 1 Corinthians 3:16

This Kingdom business that I talk about happens on the outside of the confines of the doors of the church. It's the people that we should be reaching for Christ. They are the ones that are being saved and are being added to the Kingdom. And these are the people who are building the Kingdom.

I realized that preachers have no problem putting messages together with all the points and then tell stories of their escapades, how they laid hands on this one and how this one was healed. How this one did that, and how devils came out, and about how all these things happened, but that was then, what about now? I see nothing happening. We need to quit talking and start producing. It's just all talk, no actions.

I'm convinced that the church needs to be transformed back into the image of Christ. Somewhere along the line we lost our purpose of what we were supposed to be doing before the end comes.

Let me give you one that I heard not long ago "doctrine without demonstration creates frustration, but when you have doctrine and demonstration, you then create transformation." I believe that this is what we are supposed to be doing, and that is transforming people's lives from sin to purpose.

> *For we are God's handiwork, created in Christ Jesus to do good works, which God prepared in advance for us to do.* Ephesians 2:10

That's another thing. People seem to forget that there is an end. He is coming back to take his church home, but have we become so fleshly that we can't discern what is real and what is fake?

> *Do not conform to the pattern of this world, but be transformed by the renewing of your mind. Then you will be able to test and approve what God's will is — his good, pleasing and perfect will.* Romans 12:2

> *This know also, that in the last days perilous times shall come.* 2 TIMOTHY 3:1 (NKJV)

I know we've seen some hard times, but I don't think we've seen the perilous times that the scripture is talking about. It is yet to come. I love it when I hear a preacher talking about this great revival that's coming. I talked about this and clarified what a true revival and just a meeting is.

I think that's already happened and I think we'll see breakouts here and there. If you preach the Word, somebody's going to hear it and believe it. But I'm more concerned with these perilous times that the scripture talks about in 2 Timothy that people are going to have to go through. It's not going to be easy.

I am talking about people dying in the streets with their blood flowing into the gutters. People if there ever was a time where we need THE CHURCH, it's now. I am not talking about a place that makes you feel good. I'm talking about a place where the messages that the pastors are preaching are corrective words that will get us in line for the season that is coming. If there ever was a time when you're going to need the Lord, it's now.

CHAPTER 3:
Call to The Watchman

I keep looking for the church, but for some reason I can't find it. I see buildings with names come in here go in with us, we have it. But then you drive down the street, and there's another sign that says come here, we have it. I begin to believe that there's nobody there that does have it, until we are willing to go back to the old way. Wow, all of a sudden, I have such a wave of the Holy Spirit.

Think about this, "You are deceived because you have drunk the Kool-Aid" this is what He is saying to me. "When I see the blood, I will pass over you." Do you get it? Until He sees the blood. It's the only thing that matters. You can have all the smoke and mirrors, all the multimedia extravaganzas, you can put together a great show, but it's really all about the BLOOD and the shedding of His Blood.

If you abide in me, and my words abide in you, ask whatever you wish, and it will be done for you. By this my Father is glorified, that you bear much fruit and so prove to be my disciples. JOHN:16:7-8 (ESV)

The 2024 election was one of the most important elections that we've seen, at least in my lifetime, and the way that it happened in the way that this man won the election. It had to have been orchestrated by God. I believe it was at some point that the church began to pray and was seriously seeking God's face. Because of that God spoke, and moved for the Church, but then self-love and self-gratification entered in. This may be one of the worst things that gets into a Christians life.

As I was praying, God spoke this to me, or spoke to my spirit, immediately after this man won the election.

The church went back to sleep now that this man is in office. We made him our savior, but can I tell you, he's just a man. For sure he's the right man for this time, but he is still just a man.

The man, the President, and the Senate, and the House of Representatives these individuals are not the ones that are actually running the government. We're always hearing about the swamp, and this is true, but I'm convinced that there is a shadow government that we don't see. This shadow government is calling all the shots and what the Church doesn't realize is that these individuals do not want peace. They want war.

If you were to read The Communist Manifesto you would begin to realize what these men's objectives really are. Most of these men are billionaires but that's not enough. They want to be in control. It's not only money, but the world. It's all about what they can acquire at your expense. It would be so great if we woke up.

As the old saying goes, to stop and smell the roses, but I'm not sure that's going to happen anytime soon. We have seen breakouts here and there of unrest. We've seen scrimmages where individuals have tried to take over cities and streets, but the thing that is coming is not easy for me to say. I believe that we will see blood in the streets. Church, I believe it's coming, I believe we'll see it.

My heart aches, not because of myself but because of my children and my grandchildren and my great grandchildren because of what they are about to inherit. What we, the adult church, are leaving them. May God help us.

I also believe there is a great possibility of a civil war, not in Europe, but here in America. This is what we are leaving our children. It would be great if the Church would wake up but based on what I have seen to this point, I don't think there is much hope for the Church.

RELIGIOUS ENTRAPMENT

We who are called the church lost control a long time ago. We are more concerned about how many people we can get in the church building, how much money we can raise, and how big a ministry we can build. Those are the things that are important now. It's not about souls; it's about bodies filling the seats.

There is a word we need to talk about here called conviction, which is a lost word in the Church today, but what I ask next may hurt. Are you willing to see your children and the ones you love die? I'm convinced that this war is coming. With the present administration there may be a short reprieve, but be assured, it is going to happen. There will be blood in the streets.

I'm convinced that I am a watchman. By no means do I think I'm the only one. I think there are many who are called to be watchmen. I'm just not sure that the church even knows what the watchman does and how important they are for the safety and security of the body of Christ.

27

Watchmen in the Bible were guards responsible for protecting towns and military installations from surprise enemy attacks and other potential dangers. Ancient Israelite cities would station watchmen on high walls or in watchtowers.

Their job was to keep watch and warn the townspeople of pending dangers. The Hebrew word translated "watchmen" means "one who looks out,"

A watchman is one who watches. Sometimes a watchman is a scout who looks out for approaching friends, as well as enemies.

There are many references to watchmen who keep an eye out for physical threats in the Bible, as the watchmen who stood on the tower in Jezreel and saw the company of Jehu.

The watchman on the tower of Jezreel saw Jehu and his company approaching, so he shouted to Joram, "I see a company of troops coming! "Send out a rider to ask if they are coming in peace," King Joram ordered.
2nd KINGS 9:17 (NLT)

The Bible also refers to watchmen in a spiritual sense, God appointed prophets as spiritual watchmen over the souls of His people:

"Son of man, I have made you a watchman for the people of Israel; so hear the word I speak and give them warning from me." EZEKIEL 3:17

We must realize the Prophet's job as watchman was to urge God's people to live faithfully and warn them of the perils that lay ahead of them, especially in falling away into evil. We must realize that a spiritual watchman bears a heavy responsibility before the Lord. I came to the realization that the Church is unaware of the call of a watchman. Allow me the opportunity to present what it says.

Ezekiel 33 - The Watchman's Duty

> *Now the word of the Lord came to me, saying, "Son of man, speak to the sons of your people and say to them, 'If I bring a sword upon a land, and the people of the land take one man from among them and make him their watchman, and he sees the sword coming upon the land and blows the horn and warns the people, then someone who hears the sound of the horn but does not take warning, and a sword comes and takes him away, his blood will be on his own head. He heard the sound of the horn but did not take warning; his blood will be on himself. But had he taken warning, he would have saved his life. But if the watchman sees the sword coming and does not blow the horn and the people are not warned, and a sword comes and takes a person from them, he is taken away for his wrongdoing; but I will require his blood from the watchman's hand.'*

> *"Now as for you, son of man, I have appointed you as a watchman for the house of Israel; so you will hear a message from My mouth and give them a warning from Me. When I say to the wicked, 'You wicked person, you will certainly die,' and you do not speak to warn the wicked about his way, that wicked person shall die for his wrongdoing, but I will require his blood from your hand. But if you on your part*

warn a wicked person to turn from his way and he does not turn from his way, he will die for his wrongdoing, but you have saved your life.

"Now as for you, son of man, say to the house of Israel, 'This is what you have said: "Surely our offenses and our sins are upon us, and we are rotting away in them; how then can we survive?"' Say to them, 'As I live!' declares the Lord God, 'I take no pleasure at all in the death of the wicked, but rather that the wicked turn from his way and live. Turn back, turn back from your evil ways! Why then should you die, house of Israel?'

And you, son of man, say to your fellow citizens, 'The righteousness of a righteous one will not save him on the day of his offense, and as for the wickedness of a wicked one, he will not stumble because of it on the day when he turns from his wickedness; whereas a righteous one will not be able to live by his righteousness on the day when he commits sin.'

When I say to the righteous that he will certainly live, and he so trusts in his righteousness that he commits injustice, none of his righteous deeds will be remembered; but for that same injustice of his which he has committed he will die. But when I say to the wicked, 'You will certainly die,' and he turns from his sin and practices justice and righteousness, if a wicked person returns a pledge, pays back what he has taken by robbery, walks by the statutes which ensure life without committing injustice, he shall certainly live; he shall not die. None of his sins that he has committed will be remembered against him. He has practiced justice and righteousness; he shall certainly live.

"Yet your fellow citizens say, 'The way of the Lord is not right,' when it is their own way that is not right. When the righteous turns from his righteousness and commits injustice, then he shall die in it. But when the wicked turns from his wickedness and practices justice and righteousness, he will live by them. Yet you say, 'The way of the Lord is not right.' I will judge each of you according to his ways, house of Israel."

Now in the twelfth year of our exile, on the fifth of the tenth month, the survivor from Jerusalem came to me, saying, "The city has been taken." Now the hand of the Lord had been upon me in the evening before the survivors came. And He opened my mouth at the time they came to me in the morning; so my mouth was opened and I was no longer speechless.

Then the word of the Lord came to me, saying, "Son of man, they who live in these ruins in the land of Israel are saying, 'Abraham was only one, yet he possessed the land; so to us who are many the land has been given as a possession.'

Therefore say to them, 'This is what the Lord God says: "You eat meat with the blood in it, raise your eyes to your idols as you shed blood. Should you then possess the land? You rely on your sword, you commit abominations, and each of you defiles his neighbor's wife. Should you then possess the land?"' You shall say this to them: 'This is what the Lord God says: "As I live, those who are in the places of ruins certainly will fall by the sword, and whoever is in the open field I will give to the animals to be devoured, and those who are in the strongholds and in the caves will die of plague.

And I will make the land a desolation and a waste, and the pride of her power will be brought to an end; and the mountains of Israel will be deserted so that no one will pass through. Then they will know that I am the Lord, when I make the land a desolation and a waste because of all their abominations which they have committed."' "But as for you, son of man, your fellow citizens who talk with one another about you by the walls and in the doorways of the houses, speak one with another, each with his brother, saying, 'Come now and hear what the message is that comes from the Lord.'

And they come to you as people come, and sit before you as My people and hear your words, but they do not do them; for they do the lustful desires expressed by their mouth, and their heart follows their unlawful gain. And behold, you are to them like a love song by one who has a beautiful voice and plays well on an instrument; for they hear your words but they do not practice them. So when it comes — as it certainly will — then they will know that a prophet has been among them."

It's something that's not taught in most ministries. That's why I feel like a lot of people get caught up in certain situations you might even call sin, because there's nobody who feels the responsibility to be a watchman and to warn people of the pitfalls, that just come in life itself.

Jesus said to him, "I am the way, the truth, and the life. No one comes to the Father except through Me. "If you had known Me, you would have known My Father also; and from now on you know Him and have seen Him."
JOHN 14:6,7 (NKJV)

We seem to think in this day that, if we just say the words that's enough to get us to heaven, but I'm telling you, it's not enough.

That if thou shalt confess with thy mouth the Lord Jesus, and shalt believe in thine heart that God hath raised him from the dead, thou shalt be saved. For with the heart man believeth unto righteousness; and with the mouth confession is made unto salvation. Romans 10:9-10

The word conviction is very important. The Lord has to draw us and where there is no drawing, there is no conviction. I know this seems hard, but it's the truth and we must live by His Word.

It bothers me that we have things that are important, but we allow them to fall by the side, like at the altar. I was just thinking the other day, I can go right now to the very place where I found the Lord as a young boy of 12. I can go to Raysville Baptist Church in Moore County Tennessee, the altar is still there, the place on the right side of that bench where I knelt and stayed until the Lord took away my sins.

This is important.

We must get back to that place "The Altar" though most churches have taken it out. We must bring it back. An old preacher, Brother Burt Clendenton once said "THE FIRE WILL NOT FALL ON AN EMPTY ALTAR" and this is so true.

The blood shall be a sign for you, on the houses where you are. And when I see the blood, I will pass over you, and no plague will befall you to destroy you, when I strike the land of Egypt. EXODUS 12:13(NKJV)

I put this Scripture here for a purpose to get the point across that when He sees the blood, He will pass over you "CHURCH"! It's still all about the blood.

What if I were to tell you that when the streets are covered with blood, that if we are saved, and covered by His blood, HE WILL PASS OVER YOU.

That if the Blood of Jesus has been applied to your life, it will not just save you , but in times of peril, it is His shed blood that will protect us, just as it makes us His.

Due to the past election, I think that this nation has been given an opportunity to correct a lot of things that are wrong in the church today.

We will have the ability to straighten it out. We must first understand that the world cannot change the world. Only the church can change what's wrong in this nation.

Righteousness exalts a nation, but sin is a disgrace to any people. Proverbs 14:34

I personally believe that the man elected was the man that God intended to be in the White House, but he is not the answer.

I believe that the church has gone back to sleep thinking that one man can correct everything that is wrong.

But the church is still the answer. The only answer: And that rests my case.

No one can come to Me unless the Father who sent Me draws him; and I will raise him up at the last day.
JOHN 6:44 (NKJV)

Then Jesus said to those Jews who believed Him, "If you abide in My word, you are My disciples indeed. And you shall know the truth, and the truth shall make you free."
JOHN 8:31, 32 (NKJV)

CHAPTER 4:
The State of The Church

I was passing through a building in the town where I live, and I heard that a church had just leased it. They began painting the front of the building. Guess what. They are painting it, yes you guessed it, a dark gray, almost black for some reason. I just don't believe that God is a God of darkness, but a God of light.

Ministries are strange today. They call them seeker-sensitive, but they're not sensitive. Especially to the needs of the people. At least that's what I find them to be.

For a minute, let's talk about the churches that are out there now. Take for instance, the seeker sensitive ministry. You can come to that church and sit there day after day, week after week, month after month, year after year. You can come to this church, and they will make you feel comfortable.

They won't challenge you with the meat of the Word but simply milk, or maybe pablum. This is what babies get fed. They will teach you things and make you think you're growing, and make you think that you're being discipled, and yet you're not receiving anything of value. Then they will put you in a small group, and this just becomes a place where you drink coffee and eat donuts. Soon this small group becomes disgruntled and eventually breaks away, and they start a church like the one they just left and this is sad.

The New Age Church

This movement includes ideas about reincarnation, the Higher Self, and soul groups. New Age literature often emphasizes that humans are responsible for the events that happen to them in life.

You will find humanist individuals with humanistic views. We find it in a lot of new age believers.

The Z Generation

Let's look at the Celebrate Recovery programs. I don't believe that they have been significantly studied, and so there is no direct evidence regarding the impact or efficacy of these programs. I do know that Detox.net gave their statistics, but yet I have not found them to be proven. Being a counselor with an associate's degree as a Christian counselor, with a minor in Christian education, I have found that the 12-step program, which is a part of celebrate recovery, only works if you work the 12 steps. Once you quit working the 12 steps, you revert to the old nature.

Only God can heal you completely from alcohol and chemical dependency. I have looked at most of the programs out there and I believe there are some good programs out there that do work. Let me share with you what I found so that you don't think I am giving a single opinion.

> My people are destroyed for lack of knowledge. Since you have rejected knowledge, I also will reject you from being My priest. Since you have forgotten the Law of your God, I also will forget your children. Hosea 4:6

"Celebrate Recovery (CR) faces criticism for its application of 12-step principles to broader issues beyond addiction, potential misinterpretations of Scripture, and lack of professional qualifications among its leaders. Some argue that the program's language and focus on "hurts, habits, and hangups" can obscure the role of sin and direct individuals away from a purely Christ-centered solution. Additionally, concerns exist about the potential for blame-shifting and the emphasis on performance-based accolades through the "chip system"

SPECIFIC CRITICISMS: Misapplication of 12step model: Celebrate Recovery extends the 12-step model, traditionally used for addiction, to encompass a wider range of issues like grief, codependency, and emotional trauma, which some view as inappropriate.

Misinterpretation of Scripture: Concerns exist about CR's use of Scripture, particularly the Beatitudes, in ways that may distort their original meaning and context.

Lack of Qualified Leaders: The program's leaders, typically individuals with personal experience in a 12-step program and a training retreat, are not always equipped to address complex mental health issues, according to critics.

Focus on "Hurts, Habits, and Hangups": Some argue that this terminology can distract from the core issue of sin and point individuals away from a Christ-centered solution.

Potential for Blame-Shifting: The emphasis on examining past hurts and experiences can, in some cases, lead to blame-shifting rather than taking personal responsibility for current behaviors.

The "Chip System": The system of public recognition for milestones can create a performance-based environment that some view as a distraction from genuine spiritual growth.

Lack of Crosstalk: The prohibition of crosstalk during open sharing in CR group meetings can limit opportunities for deeper connection and feedback, as noted in some studies."

The only sure programs out there are the Biblical based programs that use the word. **Faith based programs always work.**

DO NOT MISUNDERSTAND ME, I know that God will work in any program He wants. I am just sharing my experience. Being one who in March of 1980s was dying from drug dependency, probably six months from death and with the help of my wife encouraging me to cry out to God, I did, and He delivered me. I have been delivered not only from drugs, but also cigarettes and I have never reverted to either drugs, or the cigarette addiction. If you want to, you can see more of my testimony on my website **https://www.DrGaryRay.com**

Most of those programs can medicate you and get you through an episode, but I am a firm believer, and I know there are those who will disagree with me, that only God can heal a person. One of the reasons why I say that is because I am one who God has healed.

I have never had a relapse since the night that I came back to God, and He delivered me and set me free. At some point we must come back to God. You may ask why I went through all of this. The reason is simply I made bad choices. I assure you the devil (alone) didn't make me do it. It was absolutely my choice and God's test. And the same is true concerning the church.

The Church is in the condition that it is in, because of the choices that the church has made.

I don't know if you realize it or not, but the church has become controlled by reconstructionist. They want to rebuild the church to fit their deceitful desires, even allowing sin to take place in the church.

I guess this is as good a place as any to name those sins. Let's start with:

- Abortion, which is murder.
- Homosexuality, same sex marriages.
- Taking children out of the hands of the parents.
- Allowing schools to have drag queens come and read books to them, convincing our children that if they want to change their gender, they can do this without the parents knowing it.

It is my opinion that this is an abomination to God. Just think, we have aborted or killed over 1 million babies this year alone. These are the very things our forefathers preached against. I have said it would lead to the destruction of our nation, and I guess that's what is happening right before our eyes. And I am convinced that before it ends, we will see "BLOOD IN THE STREETS."

And because of the pandemic we saw a lot of rotting in the streets in and an attempt to take over certain cities. And the fact that people seem to want this critical race theory to be a reality, and they want to get rid of the police. Please, my Christian brothers, understand this is what they want us to accept, and for us to believe, but it's not the truth.

First, we don't hate our black brothers, or our Hispanic brothers, or our Asian brothers. We love everyone, so I pray that we wake up before it's too late, and we end up like Venezuela or Cuba.

I also have become aware that based on everything that is going on, the liberals are intent on creating World War III and the destruction of the world as we know it. Here are a few things that have led up to this

Let's take a look at the church for just a moment. Right now, the church is giving birth to a baby named Ichabod, the spirit of the Lord has departed this place. You see the church has been left in the hands of leaders that never had a father to raise them up spiritually

> *He said to them, "The Scriptures declare, 'My Temple will be called a house of prayer for all nations, 'but you have turned it into a den of thieves."* MARK 11:17-18 (NLT)

When the leading priest and teachers of religious law heard what Jesus had done, they began planning how to kill him. But they were afraid of him because the people were so amazed at his teaching.

The other night, as I was praying and seeking God, He gave me a spiritual definition for a reprobate mind. It is when people's brains become detached from reality and begin to believe the garbage the liberals are spewing out.

Let me show you what God is looking for:

WE FIND IT IN HIS WORD

That he might present it to himself a glorious church, not having spot, or wrinkle, or any such thing; but that it should be holy and without blemish. Ephesians 5:27 (GB)

In whom we have redemption through his blood, the forgiveness of sins, according to the riches of his grace; Ephesians 1:7 (GB)

Let me ask you a hard question here:

WHO CAN'T BE SAVED?

You might think this has nothing to do with this book, but it does.

For it is impossible for those who were once enlightened, and have tasted the heavenly gift, and have become partakers of the Holy Spirit, if they fall away, to renew them again to repentance, since they crucify again for themselves the Son of God, and put Him to an open shame. HEBREWS 6:4-6

GARY RAY
MINISTRIES

42

CHAPTER 5:
The State of the State

US border authorities encountered more than 2 million migrants, some of whom repeatedly tried to cross the border, in fiscal year 2022, according to newly released US Customs and Border Protection data. In the 2023 fiscal year, there were more than 2.4 million apprehensions at the Southwest border and more than 3.2 million encounters nationwide.

STARTLING STATS FACTSHEET:

- Fiscal Year 2024 ends with nearly 3 million inadmissible encounters
- 10.8 million total encounters since FY2021

Gangs coming across the border include

- MS-13
- Tren de Aragua (TdA)
- Other new crime syndicates

HOUSTON, Texas — More than 100 suspected members of Tren de Aragua (TdA) were a part of the group that violently stormed the border at El Paso, Texas in March. What I am saying is that the picture is not pretty. The only hope for America is for the church to come back to Christ.

If you were to read "The Communist Manifesto", you could see what is happening to our nation.

Here is just a summary.

"The Communist Manifesto", originally titled "Manifesto of the Communist Party" (German: Manifest der Kommunistischen Partei), is an 1848 political pamphlet written by German philosophers Karl Marx and Friedrich Engels. It was commissioned by the Communist League, an international political party based in London.

Here's a breakdown of its key themes and impact:

Historical Analysis of Class Struggle: The Manifesto argues that all recorded history is a history of class struggles. It traces the evolution of society through different modes of production, highlighting the inherent exploitation within each, particularly in the capitalist system of the time. It emphasizes that the capitalist system relies on the exploitation of the working class (the proletariat) by the ruling class (the bourgeoisie).

Critique of Capitalism: Marx and Engels analyze the capitalist mode of production, exposing what they viewed as its inherent contradictions and tendencies towards exploitation and alienation of the working class. They argue that capitalism doesn't offer humanity the possibility of self-realization and instead leads to stunted growth and alienation.

The Role of the Proletariat: The Manifesto positions the proletariat as the revolutionary force capable of overthrowing capitalism and establishing a classless society, which is communism.

Call for Revolution: The document explicitly calls for workers of the world to unite and overthrow the capitalist system, ending with the famous slogan, "Workers of the world, unite! You have nothing to lose but your chains".

Shift from Utopian to Scientific Socialism: The Manifesto signifies a shift from earlier forms of socialism (often termed "utopian socialism") to "scientific socialism", characterized by its systematic analysis of socio-economic relations. Marx and

Engels aimed to provide a theoretical foundation and practical program for the advancement of international communism.

Transitional Policies: The Manifesto also outlines a series of transitional policies aimed at achieving communism, including:

- Abolition of private property in land and inheritance.
- Introduction of a progressive income tax.
- Centralization of credit, communication, and transport in the hands of the state.
- Expansion and integration of industry and agriculture under state control.
- Enforcement of universal obligation of labor.
- Provision of universal education and elimination of child labor.

Impact and Legacy: "The Communist Manifesto" has had an undeniable and massive impact on the European labor movement, socialist theory, and political practice throughout the 19th and 20th centuries. It inspired political movements and revolutions worldwide, including the Russian Revolution, and became a foundational text for socialist and communist parties. It also influenced the development of modern political thought and continues to be relevant in discussions of capitalism and class struggle.

Critiques and Controversies: Despite its influence, the Communist Manifesto, and the ideas it presents have faced significant criticism. Some critics argue that the materialist conception of history is overly deterministic and simplifies complex social phenomena. The implementation of Marxist ideas in communist states has also been criticized for leading to authoritarianism and economic inefficiencies. Some argue that the predictions about the imminent collapse of capitalism, as outlined in the Manifesto, proved to be incorrect.

In essence, "The Communist Manifesto" is a powerful and influential document that presented a radical critique of capitalism and advocated for a revolutionary transformation into a classless communist society. Its analysis of class struggle and capitalism continues to be debated and studied, influencing discussions on social inequality, class structures, and power relations in the modern world.

I feel that the only way that we can take our country back is to get rid of our socialist views and again to allow the church to become the center of our life.

CHAPTER 6:
Putting First Things First

Prior to my wife passing we went to the hospital after passing out several times. After seeing her primary care doctor, she was instructed to go immediately to the emergency room.

They found out that she had two issues. One, her liver was not emptying, and it seemed to be a blockage, also there was a problem with her kidneys. The right one was swollen and the hospital in our hometown could not help her with the problem because she has a pacemaker.

She was transferred to Vanderbilt in Nashville who had the facility that could handle her problem. What I want to get across to you is that I've heard most of my life that life is in the blood. Dealing with this situation, I watched them take tube after tube of blood and I realized at that time that the doctors took the blood so that they could find the answers to the problems. It made me realize that the blood has all of the answers to the solution of my wife's problems.

Wow, life is truly in the blood. Now I will tell you, I did not like the answer that we got from the doctors. They diagnosed my wife with pancreatic cancer, but without the blood, we would never have had the diagnosis. We don't always like what we get, but we always get the true answer from the blood. Wow that makes a lot of sense, doesn't it?

After all was said and done, my wife looked at me and said "honey we have always been faithful people. Why should we stop now? God is still in control."

For the life of the flesh is in the blood, and I have given it for you on the altar to make atonement for your souls, for it is the blood that makes atonement by the life. LEVITICUS 17:11(ESV)

I keep thinking someday that we might learn the truth in God's Word. As I keep looking at the news; how easily I become discouraged at what I see going on in the world today, like the fact that parents are losing their rights to raise their children in accordance with God's word.

They are being called domestic terrorists. And the teachers are allowed to determine what gender a student should be. If they're a girl and want to be a boy, or if they're a boy, and want to be a girl, the teacher has the right to do without the parents' permission and allow this child to mutilate their body. I'm aware of something. At some point they're going to realize that someone allowed them to make the worst mistake of their life.

And then I see the church sitting by and not taking a stand and allowing this to go on in the land of the free home of the brave. It doesn't seem that phrase has much meaning anymore. State judges are being allowed to change the meaning of the law just because it suits their purpose.

I always thought that judges were to interpret the law not to reset the meaning to suit their agenda. I thought the President of this nation was still the President, but it doesn't seem that's true anymore. The man has proven that he knows exactly what he's doing and what works, and the country is going to be in a much better shape if he is allowed to continue his agenda. He was placed in office and has proven that there are the men and women for the job.

I often wonder when the church might wake up and realize that it's not the world that has the answer, but it's us, the church that has the only answer and solution to the problems of this world.

I remember, and I'm not sure if this program is still running on TV. It was called "As the World Turns." I always call it "As the Stomach Turns" it's a true picture of the world and the church. I talked about it in the last chapter. Parents' rights have been stolen from them. Losing the right to raise their children the way that they desire, based on their religious beliefs. Most of the rights have been stolen by LBGTQ rights.

Let me establish a fact, I am a Christian conservative. I was watching the news and became aware that we're very easily at the beginning of the end. I do think that the President has set in motion things that will begin to straighten out our country. I'm just not sure there's enough time, the President installed men and women who were more than qualified to do the jobs that need to be done, but it's not enough.

The opposing party became irate and some of those even in the House of Representatives were upset at several men who were brought in to look for how much money had been wasted. They are trying to recoup it so that they can begin to pay down the national debt.

Some of them have become violent because they don't want the money to be found. They are taking one of these individuals that they disapprove of and are targeting his company.

They're destroying his product and hurting innocent people, the ones who bought the products and they're doing harm to their product and destroying their things.

It has become really scary. They are planning riots, they say they are going to be peaceful, but I doubt very seriously that they will remain peaceful. I think one of the things that really concerns me is that some of these people will be angry, marching and rioting. There will be people you will see in church on Sunday morning thinking that everything they have done was OK.

I'm sorry, this is not what God intended for His church to be like. In the beginning He established the family. I'm convinced that the scripture is true, you cannot serve man and mammon.

> *No one can serve two masters, for either he will hate the one and love the other, or he will be devoted to the one and despise the other. You cannot serve God and money.*
> Matthew 6:24 (ESV)

Well, I have a lot to say, especially to the church. It's time for us, as a body of believers, to put on our big boy pants and quit expecting someone else to do what we ourselves can do. We played the game too long. If we were allowed to win again and get back, we're going to have to get busy and change things.

First, we need to preach the message of salvation. There are so many sitting in the church today that have never really been saved. They think they're OK but they're really not.

Second, we must learn again how to pray. Not just praying a prosperity message or a feel-good message but praying for God to move. Not only in our personal life, but in the life of those in the church.

Third, in order for us to become a fisher of men, we must first learn that no one can do my job better than me, so let's get busy. It's time to bring the church back to its former glory.

I really do think that it's moving day for the church. We've been in a daze far too long. So, what did the scripture say in 2nd Chronicles 7:14 (ESV)

"If my people who are called by my name humble themselves, and pray and seek my face and turn from their wicked ways, then I will hear from heaven and will forgive their sin and heal their land."

Notice first what He does in the Scripture. He identifies who He's talking to, they are His people who are known by His name and the Scripture. Also let us look, only those whom He knows He will call out. It would be a scary thought to be called out and for Him to say; depart from Me you worker of iniquities, because I never knew you. From that point there will be no way of coming back, because when He says depart, you will depart.

I want to be sure. I want to be one of those that He calls to join Him. I don't want to be left out, and I do realize all that we have to do to be counted in that number is to be saved. Be assured. Can you do your job? It can only be done by you so, when are you going to quit making excuses and just do what God is calling you to do?

We need called men and women in the gospel right now! We really are lacking truly called individuals. Instead, we have a lot of hirelings.

"I am the good shepherd. The good shepherd gives His life for the sheep. But a hireling, he who is not the shepherd, one who does not own the sheep, sees the wolf coming and leaves the sheep and flees; and the wolf catches the sheep and scatters them. JOHN 10:11-12 (NKJV)

CHAPTER 7:
Be Ready

These are the things that I say, or things that I feel, so please sit back and put your seatbelt on. Get ready!

As a young boy growing up, I can't remember what the church really looked like. I just wanted church to be over, so I could get home. Then there was a time when I was about 12 years old, when I really had an experience with the Lord. It was at a Sunday night meeting. Brother Bryce Holder was preaching. I remember he preached so hard and had wept as he preached, so his shirt was totally soaked. He made a couple of statements that really got my attention as a young boy. Then I let go, went to the altar and was gloriously saved.

When these things really happen, you don't easily forget them. No, let me correct that, you don't ever forget them. The problem is, so many today are sitting in a few of our churches and have never had a true experience with the Lord.

Let's take a look at where the church and Christians as a whole stand first. I would like for you to see the scripture.

> *Woe to those who call evil good, and good evil; Who put darkness for light, and light for darkness; Who put bitter for sweet, and sweet for bitter!* ISAIAH 5:20 (NKJV)

After seeing what is transpiring in our world today, and with the news media, some are good, some are not so good. Looking at the scripture above, it talks about calling evil good, and good evil.

I believe that's what we see now in our country, with the fact that we have left leaning, socialist Democratic Senators and Representatives who are our calling evil good, and good, evil.

And you question, why do I say this? Didn't a group of Senators and Representatives go to El Salvador to petition for someone who came into this country illegally? He was also a known member of an El Salvador gang that has been very brutal in our country. He is also a well-known wife beater and yet they want him to be brought back and released. It just doesn't make sense to me.

I conclude, that if we would simply read the written Word, the Bible gives us a view of everything that not only is going to happen but is happening before our eyes. Sometimes it's a little bit scary to see it manifesting before our eyes.

The Word lets us know that it's not going to get any better. It says it's going to worsen every day. I'll tell you I'm convinced that we will see blood in the streets.

I have my own eschatological beliefs, but I concluded that it doesn't matter, we just must be ready when it comes. In the end it will come, and we will go to Heaven or Hell. We can't pray for someone who has passed or buy someone out of torment. Heaven is eternal, and so is Hell. Things will get bad, but this isn't Hell.

It grieves me to watch people who know better, but continue to allow American people to be hurt, and killed by illegal individuals whom the Democratic Party allowed in. I think we must wake up, I'm smelling something, but it isn't the roses.

But when you hear of wars and commotions, do not be terrified; for these things must come to pass first, but the end not immediately." LUKE 21:9 (NKJV)

Not too long ago, I heard a preacher say:

"GET READY, GET READY, GET READY."

So, I am convinced that the church must keep their eyes open, and find Jesus, because His return is imminent. I'm saying, I am perplexed it is like walking into nothing but total darkness. And to be satisfied with it.

I never thought that I would see the day, even though I read it in the Bible, that the very elect might be deceived. And I do believe this deception is taking place now. If we were to just open our eyes and look at this world through our spiritual glasses, it might wake us up to the reality in time.

Everyone will deceive his neighbor and will not speak the truth; they have taught their tongue to speak lies; they weary themselves to commit iniquity. JEREMIAH 9:5 (NKJV)

"Then if anyone says to you, 'Look, here the Christ!' or 'There!' do not believe for a false christ and false prophets will rise and show great signs and wonders to deceive, if possible, even the elect (and I am one of those that believes that they can) . *See, I have told you beforehand.* MATTHEW 24:23-25 (NKJV)

I have just given you two scriptures, one from the old and one from the New Testament. There are many more Scriptures in the Bible, if you simply look, that speak of the destruction that is to come.

Now I know that there are false prophets out there today, and they are saying "don't worry everything is OK."

I must tell you; everything is not OK. When you see people that you thought could never be deceived and people that you thought were godly people believing in the lies, its scary folks, but it's real. I know that at some point in this book a lot of people will just put it down and call it heresy. But at my age that doesn't bother me anymore. The thing that bothers me is that there are people being deceived today, and if I can change just one life, hearing what I have to say, as hard as it may seem, it will be worth it.

Any of this could happen now, or take place at any moment, which to me is very frightening. That is to see the "regression" not the progression of the church. Looking back at when the pandemic happened, we realize that this is something that was perpetrated for a purpose.

Now I understand some of the things I am about to say are from my perspective, not necessarily anyone else's. I watched how easily things began to happen, and how easy it was to convince the church to close its doors, and how easy it was to convince the people to stay at home.

By the way, there was a church that closed its doors during the pandemic, and they lost about 300 members. After they released the church to open their doors those 300 people never came back to church.

Next what we saw happen particularly in some western states, people began to take over the streets and set up their little towns and communities in the streets. They would raid the stores and steal whatever they wanted and beat people up. Some were killed.

It was just horrendous what we witnessed at that time. I must tell you that these are things that are soon to come. I believe that it will get a lot worse. I am writing to let people know that there will be blood in the streets. You can call it World War III if you want or just a war, I don't believe it will be fought in Europe or some foreign country, I believe it will be here in the streets where we live.

Let's go just a little bit further. Recently, in Africa a preacher was pulled out of his pulpit and taken to prison. Now they got him out, and he was able to come home, but I am afraid there's a time when church doors will be closed again and preachers will be pulled from their pulpit and marred, even in front of their congregations.

I know that's a scary thought, but there is a distinct possibility that this will happen. We pray that just maybe, your church would take on the character of God again before all of this happens. I'm just not sure if it's possible. God never gives or equips anyone without accountability.

My desire is that something that I might say in this book would get the church's attention and call people to wake up, and to realize what's happening to our country today. I know some of the things that I've said to this point seem very hard, but I feel they're true.

I don't back down from anything that I have said. I do know that the only way it's going to work, is when this nation comes back to God. Not part of the way. I have talked many times about the fact that the only piece of furniture in a church that really matters is the altar and most churches have taken it out.

Most of us who have truly found the Lord understand that you can make an altar anywhere but just remember that the building that's called the Church; if you were to strike a match to it, it would immediately burn to the ground. The only thing that has value is the altar and most churches have taken it out.

AGAIN, I repeat, there was an old man who said that,

"THE FIRE WILL NOT FALL ON AN EMPTY ALTAR"

I hate to say this, but I firmly believe that the church has invited sin in, and anytime the devil is invited, he'll come right on in. Today it's no different than the world.

Everything is OK but I can remember the day that sin in the church, or around the church was not OK and that experience meant something, it's conviction that causes an actual change in their lives.

I hope and pray that some of this gets through to them. There is one thing that really troubles me, I became aware of the fact that there are so many different views on who the devil is, they can't even agree on what his name really is or even how much power he really has.

We do know that he is an enemy who the scripture says.

> *The thief does not come except to steal, and to kill, and to destroy. I have come that they may have life, and that they may have it more abundantly.* JOHN 10:10

He is an enemy of the church, and anything that pertains to spirituality. In the beginning, he set out to destroy the one thing that God created, and that is family. He thinks that if he can stop the family or destroy the family that can change everything, and he can win in the end. We know that's impossible, and I know he knows that, but he never stops trying. We know that someday God will say, "go bring my children home," and at that point the devil, our adversary, will go to hell to be with his angels and all those whom he deceived.

When God first came, He came as a baby but the next time He comes, He's is coming as the King of Kings and Lord of Lords!

My desire is to dedicate this book to everyone who doesn't know Him. My prayer is for anyone who reads this book that the Holy Spirit will convict them, if they're not saved, and that they'll come to the Lord. Those who know God, and who have experienced Him, that they will once again feel the Holy Spirit and come back to Him.

Now again, may this book be a blessing to someone and I pray that someone might find and accept Jesus into their life. This is my desire

"AMEN!"

Dr. Gary Ray

ABOUT THE AUTHOR

Dr. Gary Ray is on a mission; a mission to spread the Truth and Good News of Jesus Christ to everyone! A great need exists today for truth to be spoken, and he is up to the challenge. The Bible says in John 8:31-32:

To the Jews who had believed him, Jesus said, "If you hold to my teaching, you are really my disciples. Then you will know the truth and the truth will set you free."

Our modern-day society tends to bend, shy away from, or spin the truth so it will be better received, and more palatable. In many cases, the truth gets diluted to the point where the original message is non-existent but in II Timothy 4:3-4 we read:

A time is coming when people will no longer listen to sound and wholesome teaching. They will follow their own desires and will look for teachers who will tell them whatever their itching ears want to hear. They will reject the truth and chase after myths.

Does this sound familiar? Does this describe anyone you know? Does this describe what is going on in your local church? If so, they have rejected the truth and are chasing after myths.

At Gary Ray Ministries, we are committed to unapologetically teaching and preaching truth; truth that will set us free from the bondage of sin and death (John 8:34). Truth sets us free, delivers us from our captive state, and helps us realize the full potential freedom brings, but non-truth keeps us in bondage and keeps us divided.

Dr. Gary Ray knows a little something about how truth can set a person free and release them into the fullness of what God has for their lives.

As a seasoned minister, Pastor, Teacher, Apostle, and Evangelist, Dr. Gary is taking his testimony "On the Road Again!" Through his testimony, he desires to see truth proclaimed and unity restored to the Body of Christ.

OTHER BOOKS AVAILABLE
BY DR. GARY RAY

As I endeavored to put this book together, my goal was to .et us look behind the veil. Even though the curtain was rent from top to bottom, there a~e things that we should see and realize their importance about today's Church.

Dr. Gary Ray knows a thing or two about deliverance. He himself has an amazing deliverance experience and you can read all about it in his book, Deliverance: The Final Release of the Church.

In this book, Ophelia Ray tells her raw, first-hand experiences of being the wife of Dr. Gary Ray. She gives a first-hand account and the raw details of a tru ministry journey. Available now on Amazon in paperback.

Additional Books available at
www.DrGaryRay.com